Desert Lives

by Norman Stevens

Harcourt
SCHOOL PUBLISHERS

Printed in China

ISBN 10: 0-15-350684-9
ISBN 13: 978-0-15-350684-0

Ordering Options
ISBN 10: 0-15-350600-8 (Grade 3 On-Level Collection)
ISBN 13: 978-0-15-350600-0 (Grade 3 On-Level Collection)
ISBN 10: 0-15-357905-6 (package of 5)
ISBN 13: 978-0-15-357905-9 (package of 5)

11 12 13 14 15 0940 12 11 10

You look out across the desert, and the sky is blue and clear. It may be months before the sky clouds over, and it begins to rain. The Mojave [mō hä´ vē] Desert is one of the driest places on earth. It can be hot, too. On this summer morning, it is already more than 90°Fahrenheit (32°C), and it will climb to 115°Fahrenheit (46°C) later today.

As you look across the desert, nothing is moving. The ground looks rough and rugged, and the few plants you see look dead. The desert looks as if nothing could live here.

You might be surprised by all the life that is in the desert. Many plants and animals make their homes here. If you know where to look, you can find them, and you can learn how they live in a land where water is scarce.

A desert receives less than ten inches of rain in a year. We think deserts are hot, but some deserts are located in cold places. What makes a place a desert is not the heat. It is the absence of water.

There are four main desert areas in North America. The Mojave Desert lies mostly in California, and it includes the driest places in North America.

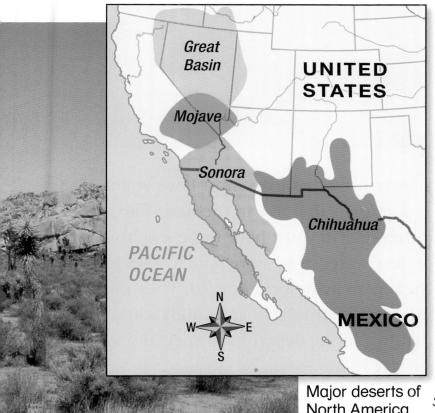

Great Basin

UNITED STATES

Mojave

Sonora

Chihuahua

PACIFIC OCEAN

N
W E
S

MEXICO

Major deserts of North America

5

Anything that lives must have water. Plants and animals that live in the desert are no different. They just have to be able to survive on less water or to store water. They must find shelters to avoid heat or cold. They must find food anywhere they can. Animals and plants that live in the desert have special ways to survive.

Many desert animals go underground to get away from the heat. The kangaroo rat lives in a burrow in the desert. During the day the kangaroo rat seals the burrow to keep out heat. Dampness from its breathing helps to keep the burrow cool. After the sun goes down, the kangaroo rat comes out of its burrow. Its eyes see well in the dim light.

The kangaroo rat's body is different from other rats. It can get water from even the driest seeds. Its body also uses more of the water it gets. It lives its whole life without ever taking a drink of water.

Many desert animals have light-colored skin that helps reflect heat rather than absorb it. The zebra-tailed lizard runs quickly across hot rocks. It sometimes holds its tail up to scare other animals. Perhaps it looks like a snake's tail. If something grabs the tail, the tail just breaks off!

Most desert animals get the water they need from the things they eat. Insects eat leaves and sometimes bore into plants to get the water that they need. When small animals, birds, or reptiles eat the insects, they get water from the insects' bodies. When larger animals eat small animals, they also get fluids. The desert tortoise gets water from the grasses and flowers it eats during spring rains. It has a special part of its body to store water for the dry season.

   Desert plants find ways to survive in the harsh desert environment, too. There are more than seven hundred types of plants in the Mojave Desert. The inside of a cactus stores water like a sponge. Many desert plants have a waxy skin that holds in water. Some plants have shallow roots to catch every bit of rain that falls in the sand. Others have deep roots that go far down into the ground where there may be water.

   Many desert plants have needles. Needles are a form of leaf that protects the plants from animals. Needles offer some shade to the skin of plants, which protects the plants from heat.

Some plants simply wait for rain, sometimes for years. When rain comes, some plants bloom. Some grow leaves. Some plant seeds have hard coats that do not open until there is enough rain for them to grow. Every so often, spring brings more rain than usual. Then the whole desert blooms. Green grasses grow, colorful flowers appear, and the desert is beautiful.

This beauty does not last because soon the water dries up. The plants return to the way they were and wait for more water.

With its rocks and spines, the desert may look tough, but it is actually a fragile place. Life is hard for things that live in the desert. It does not take much to upset the balance. Because desert plants grow very slowly, years of growth can be ruined permanently by a few careless human beings.

Humans pose the greatest threat to the desert. The edge of a city drifts into the desert where once only desert creatures lived. People dig up the land for sand and gravel. They pump out what little water is under the ground. Some drive over the land in off-road vehicles for fun, destroying animal burrows and plants.

People are also trying to save the deserts. Some desert areas have been made into protected parklands. Laws have reduced mining. Livestock that harm plants are not allowed to graze in some places. Off-road vehicles are not allowed in some areas of the desert.

The best way to protect the desert is to learn about it. You can read more books about desert plants and animals. You can tell people about the interesting creatures that live there.

Some people think the desert is empty. As you stand looking across the Mojave on a summer morning, you know better.

Think Critically

1. What is the biggest surprise about the desert?

2. Why does the kangaroo rat come out of its burrow *after* the sun goes down?

3. What happens in the desert when some rain does fall in the spring?

4. Explain ways that plants and animals get water in the desert.

5. How do you think this author would feel about riding motorcycles in the desert?

 Science

Desert Facts Some deserts are located in cold places. Find out about a desert where it is cold. Write three facts about the desert that you have chosen.

School-Home Connection The hottest temperature ever recorded in the United States was in the Mojave Desert. It was 134°Fahrenheit (56°C)! What is the highest temperature you've ever been in? Ask friends and family members to tell stories of the hottest day they have ever known.

Word Count: 916